811
B725 w
264198

*Weathers
and Edges*

PHILIP BOOTH

Weathers
and Edges

264198

NEW YORK / THE VIKING PRESS

First published in 1966 by The Viking Press, Inc.
625 Madison Avenue, New York, N.Y. 10022

Published simultaneously in Canada by
The Macmillan Company of Canada Limited

Library of Congress catalog card number: 66-15909
Printed in U.S.A. by the Vail-Ballou Press, Inc.

for DAVID BRADLEY

who homed me in
on the choice of cruising
a coast where there's
no place to hide

CONTENTS

Forecast   *1*

Choosing a Homesite   *5*
Incident in Santo Domingo   *7*
Heart of Darkness   *8*
The Day the Tide   *11*
Dry Fall   *13*
Fairy Tale   *14*
A Field of White Birds   *15*
Homesick Upstate   *17*
A Refusal of Still Perfections   *18*
Cleaning Out the Garage   *19*
He   *21*
One Man's Wife   *22*
Not as Children   *23*
Small Dance   *25*
Cider   *26*
The Dancer   *27*
Denying the Day's Mile   *28*
After the *Thresher*   *31*

Under the West Side Highway   *32*

That Clear First Morning   *34*

Deer Isle   *35*

Snow   *37*

Cynthia's Weathers   *39*

The Man on the Wharf   *41*

Five Ways of Facing the Deep

    I.   Stefansson Island   *43*

    II.   Homage   *44*

    III.   A Choice of Horizons   *45*

    IV.   Light   *47*

    V.   Sea-Change   *47*

The Sedgwick Boulder   *49*

The Ship   *53*

Refusing the Sea   *57*

Voyages   *59*

Report from the Scene   *60*

Seaweed   *62*

Tenants' Harbor   *63*

Offshore   *65*

ACKNOWLEDGMENTS

My thanks to the editors of the following periodicals for having first printed most of these poems, many in earlier versions:

The Atlantic Monthly	*The New Republic*
The Carleton Miscellany	*The New York Review of*
Epoch	*Books*
Harper's Magazine	*Poetry Northwest*
The Hudson Review	*The Saturday Review*
The Humanist	*Shenandoah*
Jeopardy	*Syracuse 10*
The Kenyon Review	*The Virginia Quarterly Review*
The Massachusetts Review	*Voices*

Also to *The New Yorker* for "Tenants' Harbor" and "Sea-Change" (originally published as "Marin," and here reprinted from my earlier book *The Islanders*); and to *Poetry* for "The Dancer," "Refusing the Sea," and "That Clear First Morning" (originally published as "August 1942").

I am also grateful to the editors of *Best Poems of 1963, The New York Times Book Review,* and *Mind and Destiny* (Syracuse University Press), in which some of these poems were earlier reprinted; and to the editors of *The Distinctive Voice* (Scott, Foresman & Company), in which two of the poems first appeared.

I don't know how to say adequate thanks to the John Simon Guggenheim Memorial Foundation, which gave me a sense of the freedom these poems mean to return. Nor do I know words for the share that Kim, Cal, Priscilla, Alvin, and George have in this book; they, and Margaret most of all, were first with criticism and courage.

—P.B.

FORECAST

The late fog, lifting.
A first wind, risen.
The long tide, at ebb.

And cast off finally,
into that perfect hope,
the fishboats: going out.

Weathers
and Edges

CHOOSING A HOMESITE

If possible, choose a lot
not already surveyed
for next fall's Thruway, not

this spring to be conveyed
to the Commissioner of Parks,
or on the Instrument

Approach of Mach-3 jets
(although your own rights
will be, always, defended

in any case of Eminent
Domain, or Public Works)
when the next runway is extended.

Since conscience might, of course,
commit you to a new State
Asylum, you could do worse,

in truth, than finance a lot
in some strategically optioned, still-
to-be-paved development; a last

choice, yes, but zoned, green,
and *No Cash Down*
for paraplegic veterans. Prices

are high, but consider the cost
of moving up: say to a hill-
top thick with scanning devices.

Big fields are good, but beware
the silo housing a hybrid
missile. Search your deed,

if you choose the coast, for sub-pens
under your frontage. A lot
will depend, too, on what happens

overhead. The apple valleys,
upstate, are heavy with millicuries.
If you bear children, share

your mortgage with them: they,
or their children, will have to pay
if real estate booms. Whatever homesite

you choose, you'll be taxed to play hero.
Now that the bombsight is obsolete,
today's best buy is Ground Zero.

INCIDENT IN SANTO DOMINGO

He didn't think. He did
what he thought he ought to.

Marine to the butt, he'd
screwed their women blue;

and signed his bitching-home
with the wife-word, "Love. . . ."

This was the world he'd come
to: his privates, up the street,

taunted by men with dark skin.
"Frig 'em," he said; and did,

with his trigger finger. The heat
was bad, and he hadn't had leave

for a week. He didn't think; he
pressed what sergeants are trained to:

"I'm gonna get me a native,"
he said. He did.   *CBS*

reporting, Santo Domingo.

HEART OF DARKNESS

> *You ought to have heard him*
> *recite poetry, his own, too,*
> *it was . . . Oh, he enlarged my*
> *mind.*
> —THE HARLEQUIN SEAMAN

Exterminate the brutes.
We remember that part.
We remember Kurtz,
and his final horror.
To say he only pretended
to be of the new gang,
the gang of virtue,
is not to have read
the full Report.
Or is not to have been there.
Marlow, of course, knew.
He was there. But recall
how he had to lie,
as a matter of conscience,
to get himself back.
We know that. We, too,
have rivets and work,
science, and new
editions of *Towson's*
Inquiry to occupy
our minds. Efficiency
is what saves us.
It would be an error,
though, to imagine
that Marlow's tale

was ever conclusive.
As they knew on the *Nellie,*
counting a river
of flickering lights,
and waiting out a night
tide, there's not much
to go on: The Intended,
with her blindfold and torch,
the background near black;
and always in a white suit,
the Chief Accountant;
chained natives, dying;
popguns firing into
a continent's underbelly,
a few shrunken heads
on some pointed sticks;
and, yes, the voice—
vox clamantis—we know
all that. But the center,
the center is still elusive.
We must find the poem.
One that, again, might
enlarge our harlequin
mind. Lost as we
are, with no choice
of nightmares left,
but only stakes
higher than Kurtz
could dream of, what
we need is the poem.
Not that we'll ever

get back to where we,
in our virtue, began.
But if, at least,
we try for some coastal
station, the poem,
the poem that must
map the bottom
of here, would be
some sort of base
to start out from.

THE DAY THE TIDE

The day the tide went out,
and stayed, not just at Mean
Low Water or Spring Ebb,
but out, out all the way
perhaps as far as Spain,
until the bay was empty,

it left us looking down
at what the sea, and our
reflections on it, had
(for generations of
good fish, and wives fair
as vessels) saved us from.

We watched our fishboats ground
themselves, limp-chained in mud;
careened, as we still are
(though they lie far below us)
against this sudden slope
that once looked like a harbor.

We're level, still, with islands,
or what's still left of them
now that treelines invert:
the basin foothills rock
into view like defeated castles,
with green and a flagpole on top.

Awkward as faith itself,
heron still stand on one leg
in trenches the old tide cut;

maybe they know what the moon's
about, working its gravity
off the Atlantic shelf.

Blind as starfish, we
look into our dried reservoir
of disaster: fouled trawls, old
ships hung-up on their mon-
ument ribs; the skeletons
of which our fathers were master.

We salt such bones down with self-
consolation, left to survive,
if we will, on this emptied slope.
Réunion Radio keeps reporting
how our ebb finally flooded
the terrible Cape of Good Hope.

DRY FALL

Where no artesian drill
will clank, where dry-mouthed doubt
is older than five-months' drought,
I bend to dig with a tool
as old as the first dug well.

A withered man came to dowse
this hill: his hazel twig
twitched like a broken leg,
his hand divined what flows
under my udder-shrunk cows,

and I paid him the calf last dead.
Now, cursing my arid ridge
with a chipped steel edge,
I dig without sweat where his rod
bowed down. We've both been had

by traffic with his hard God:
his calf's as thick with poison
as my dead hope of water from stone;
the struck ledge numbs my blood
where it rocks my bone.

FAIRY TALE

Half awake, the boy in the big bed haunted
by guns sits up to fire his blank tears.
The world he dreamed was a palace, painted
blue to match the Queen's dress. There were fairs
every day. He could swim. Whenever he wanted

the animals left, and a tent slanted
over the chair where he kept her warm.
Because of the dwarf in the moat, he invented
the gun she let him have; he guarded her room
at night. Whatever he asked, she granted.

He lived there years and years: he counted
time by counting how many names
he could find for that dark, dwarf-stunted,
man in the moat, and how many times
he had killed what all those names hunted.

He dreamed all this. He dreamed that scented
Queen who'd never, ever, let him be dead.
But when he woke, he could hear, tented
over her, big as the dark of her bed,
the dwarf whose black cannon was mounted.

His fingers wanted to kill, but were blunted
with lead: a world of infinite corridors
weighted his waking, and everywhere slanted
away, away from dreaming to wars
in bed; which was not the world he wanted.

A FIELD OF WHITE BIRDS, GROUNDED; AFTER A FROZEN LUNCH IN CENTRAL NEW YORK

And you think *these*
are seagulls? You
who order Maine fish
at The Syracuse
House, and peck with
your fork, pro-
claiming it's *fresh!*

The menu says so.
So does The Bird Book,
Jack, salt these
white birds away
on its sea-stuff page.
But here they feed,
investing a frieze

of split-level corn:
colonial motels,
and ranches ranked
against snow. Gulled
like salesmen who
pooped out on a
quota, they banked

on the book or the menu,
overflew, and sit spent,
sold on insolent lives.
Upstate eats its own mort-
gages; even these gulls,
foreclosed by the sea, try
to swallow themselves.

HOMESICK UPSTATE

Leaving Don Dike's at midnight—
an unlikely farm, twentynine miles
from nowhere, in upstate New York—
I walked out under the first April stars,
the cupped moon heavy, Orion
tipped down to the hardwood hills,
and the oak on those hills lifted dark.

I could hear the croak of cold peepers
out of the shallows, the brook
by the unpainted barn running black.
I took a leak beside the parked cars.
The party was over, we'd all be sleepers
soon; the beer was good, but time
ran always downhill, running back.

I thought of the trout in that brook,
browns and rainbows nudging the dark.
It was upstate, nowhere, and midnight;
I had to go home. But my water
was part of the ground: I ran downstream
past Don Dike's dark barn,
dark where the trout swam light.

A REFUSAL OF STILL PERFECTIONS

That bare farm stripped of summer
drifts in my sleep. The river below
its field is salt, tidal, and blue.
I own how that farm rests white
on white: barn on house on snow.

But I know I can never live there.
Never, for pasture, mortgage the river,
or pawn dark hopes to insure pure sleep.
The fence behind me casts tidal shadows.
I wake to mornings I'd better keep.

CLEANING OUT THE GARAGE

for J.B.F.

Hooks, screw-eyes, and screws; the walls
thick with bent nails to catch on: somebody's
grandfather must have hoped his grandson
would use these nicked tools. Adze, spoke-shave,
and saw hang with dead moth-wings, spidered
to leaning studs. Fifty winters have heaved
this catch-all off its foundations, cracked
the poured-floor, and left to mildew the tent
I almost slept in, moored to my boyhood backyard.

Sponges that bilged three lapstrake rowboats
(the lot of them rotted or sunk) stiffen
like pockmarked soft footballs; instructions
for washing the Model-T Ford curl tacked
to the faucet plank. The wall is shelved
with paintcans left to weather, their paint
skinned like my grandfather's wrinkles. The gloss
has gone soft on his set of golfclubs: troon,
nap-iron, and niblick, bagged with balls but no
putter, their hickory shafts still true.

It's summer when I haul back to all this:
a goldfinch dead in a box of unplanted
seeds, chemicals bagged to poison the weeds
that still flourish. Stormed by the dust
of my sweeping, storm windows lean stacked
like the panes my boyhood couldn't see through.
I try to sweep out the useless stuff I still

cherish: a drugstore sloop that tipped over,
a bathtub submarine that floated between
my legs like a small sick fish; I try not
to sink in this scrap I dive to uncover.

Cars jacked-up here, in '18 and '43,
the Ford and a Chevvy, still stain the cracked floor
with drip from their oilpans; my great-
grandfather's (substitute's) Civil War sword
points North like the rusted compass my family
never trusted: in all the winters somebody
shoveled a path to this island garage,
there was gear for voyages, wars, or rebuilding;
enough to see whole generations through.
I'm game for different winters in this high summer;
a woman I loved who refused me taught me what I
mean to leave here: *how to let go what won't do.*

H E

He was fifteen. And she, Wisconsin:
rolling, vernal, a fern to the sun
who answered her green question mark.

There were fields beyond them: clover
and buttercup, paintbrush, lupin;
daisy and daisy, over and over,

under bobolink, goldfinch, and lark.
He laughed out like a jack-in-the-pulpit,
woken up from the difficult dark.

ONE MAN'S WIFE

Not that he promised not to windowshop,
or refuse free samples; but he gave up
exploring warehouse bargains, and forgot
the trial offers he used to mail away for.

After, that is, she laid on the counter what
she'd long kept hidden under the penny-candy,
and demonstrated (one up-country Sunday)
the total inventory of one wife's general store.

NOT AS CHILDREN

Not as children, but
with children's feet,
we walked downbeach
between the steep
shale cliff and sea.

From that hot picnic
noon, led back
to games, I stepped
on the stones you skipped
until, twice tricked

by your hopscotch stride,
I slid on seaweed
and sat wet. Jarred,
I watched you parade
with the gulls. You stayed

distant, dry
with laughter; and I,
unwillingly,
got up to see
the sea your way.

The rocks we stood on,
facing, were green
with urchins, and green

with tide between
us, flooding in.

"Look where we stand,"
I said, "on island
rocks. . ." You turned
to sea. ". . . And ground,
someday, to sand."

I almost caught
you: "No, not yet."
But back on the steep
mainland, our feet
climbed old and wet.

SMALL DANCE

I thought I knew, for once,
how it was with the world.

And I cannot tell you. Except
that the gray cat, who slept

on my desk all morning, curled
against waking, woke to claw

at my pipe smoke. I stretched
to catch at some meaning; my mind

began to join the small dance,
and I saw my mind, like the cat's paw,

play with pure fire: I watched
him watch the smoke dissolve,

and saw my own prehensile hands
reach out to pat the cat.

Unsatisfied, he turned, resigned
to tom-cat sleep. And that,

for both of us, was that. If
curiosity killed, we'd both be stiff;

Toms that we are, we breathe it.
Neither of us understands;

but something we could not resolve
had, for a moment, smoke to wreathe it.

CIDER

Downhill through this upland meadow,
   aster and chicory, sumac,
      poplar and apple,
distill into Fall: its cider light
opens the deepening woods, de-
      canting, through leaves, this
      stillness a hundred feet tall.

Secret in their seasonal shadow,
      chipmunk-quip, the tick
      of felled acorns, thick bees,
speak only their season's self-praise.
There is no password or resident
      God; only this upland light,
      fallen through miles of trees.

THE DANCER

The dancer mended sheep and tended fences;
he was a hung-up friend to men, a lover:
balancing love, he loved to call the dances.
No one ever turned his record over.

He was a prince among the farmer princes.
He square-danced wallflowers out of doubt,
and reeled Virginias into a consensus,
until the line he loved was all reeled out.

They named a dance for him in the dancing book;
ducking-the-oyster, solo, he dove-for-the-clam:
Who, they asked, is our best dancer? It took
one hell of a dance for him to dance *I am.*

DENYING THE DAY'S MILE

Always on clear mornings
I wake across their valley
to face the day's horizon:
quickened by my tentative
steps, I leap it like
the solo shadow of a big
jet—behind which I
am the sun.
                    By the time
dusk shrinks my neighbor's
streetcorner, and staggers
me home, I'm overcast
always: I imagine men
in the Andaman Islands
waking to fish, women
giving breast in Lhasa
to children the color of rice.
But I can never conceive
what weather they wake to, or
face those multiple hands
that bait my eye to a map.
I've never even been sure
whether they're still beginning
a day I've already lost,
or a day I haven't begun.
Even with my ear close
as a child's to waves
bounced off Afghanistan,
the Black Sea, and London,

there is too much static
to pick up children eating
fists of Tibetan snow.
Before God died, I thought
it might be fun to try
his game for a while: not
to judge the world, but simply
to listen in on how
it was getting on. Now
I couldn't bear it: I can't
even stand my neighbors,
or face myself when I go
to bed with no love left
from the day.
                Always on clear
mornings I wake intending
to walk a mile, and to hold
that mile's particulars up
to the general flight of jets,
as they pretend to climb
over human weather, and land
on cement deserts that have
nothing to do with love.
I am overcast always
for having flown to escape
wild chicory I might
have picked for my wife, the man
next door I hate, and this
lousy city that managed,

without God, to smog itself
through another November day.
If I were pilot tomorrow,
I'd fly for better weather;
but tonight I'm not even
myself: where I haven't been
is already yesterday.

AFTER THE *THRESHER*

There must be people, if
there are still people, who
somewhere yet above us

(where there are even birds)
breathe, swim, and survive
at their bright apogee

while we, under pressure,
gasp, weigh on each other,
and collapse face to face.

Even this sea-level smog
would seem like graced light
to signalmen tapping out code

from a locked hull, sounding
their own slow taps from the coast's
dark beer-can floor.

Trying to face them, we stretch
to imagine release, fail
to imagine ourselves, and try

to decompress with another
iced drink: the lawnspray squeaks,
and traffic begins to thunder

as if it were Sunday somewhere.
But we have been sunk for months,
under tons of possible air.

UNDER THE WEST SIDE HIGHWAY

The lights on Ninth Avenue green
for a hundred blocks downtown:

for a husband walking paired
wolfhounds into the wind, a girl

(sweet with coffee) talked
into love at El Faro. Under

the West Side Highway, whole beef
and raw pork hang highballed

from Texas; an ashcan bonfire
warms its six Negro hands.

The parakeets on Sutton Place
South sleep hooded: uptown's

always sleeping while one man
lugs home a cross, or drinks

his seder out of a paper bag.
For us, who steep its curbs,

night is tonight's next corner:
sirens flash where we turn

to walk it: toward food, love,
or the difficult wealth of sleep.

No matter how darkly we flop
against the city's soft belly,

we wake back into New York:
sirens flash still, like all

the old world's churchbells. Yet
the sun keeps on coming up.

THAT CLEAR FIRST MORNING

That clear first morning after,
maybe turned sixteen, I
first stayed up all night

and woke from waking
to see the sun break open,
happening to the simple world:

there were people there,
who slept while I was waking,
and were waking while I woke.

I was where they were.
There were men waking to coffee
and lunch boxes, women

tending the coffee and making
lunches. They were me.
I was there, being young.

Whoever it was I'd waited up
to meet kept coming around
the corner I kept turning,

certain and new as the sun.
Beginning with that sure morning,
I slept in having begun.

DEER ISLE

Out-island once, on a South slope
bare in March, I saw a buck
limp out of the spruce and snow
to ease his gut in a hummocky meadow.

He fed two rooted hours on the hope
of spring, browsed, and flicked back
into the trees, a big ghost
of what hunters tracked at first frost.

That was six winters ago. Today,
three hundred miles South, a commuter
trapped by a detour sign
at dusk, I trailed a reflecting line

of red arrows that took me the long way
home. Late, caught in the neuter
traffic, driven beyond where I wanted
to go, I braked by a slanted

orchard where six cars were stopped.
There were six does there, feeding on frozen
winesaps, fat and white-rumped
as the drivers who sat in their cars. One limped,

and I thought of that buck, equipped
to survive, on the island he'd chosen
to swim to. That coast, about now,
would lie gray: the raw salt snow

topping a man's hauled lobsterpots,
and sifting down through thick spruce
where the sweat on a run buck
would freeze. A man with no luck

but a gun would be hunting home cross-lots.
I was parked miles beyond choice,
miles from home on a blocked curve
in the dead mist of a thick suburban preserve.

My guts clamped. I honked my way clear,
tramping the gas toward nowhere
but where home was. My wife understood.
If I didn't go now, I never would.

SNOW

Look, it's happening
all over: the trees'

changed shape, and wind
beginning to winter.

The ground gains white
as night gains ground:

houses melt behind snow.
In one of the houses,

banked against winter,
a quiet old woman

imagines Heaven.
She tries to imagine

where seasons come from,
and where, when they melt,

the seasons go.
She asks her Un-

itarian cat,
feeding him as she

dresses for church
and her straight-backed,

cold, and familiar
white pew. He

licks himself free
of encumbered milk,

his pricked ears buoyed
by the harbor-mouth bell:

swelled by the daily
justice of tides,

anchored on rock
and floated by salt,

its bell tolls three-fold
the one cold tone

to which even cats
and their women are both

born deaf: snow
melts into the sea

in these seasons; even
the fish don't know.

THE MAN ON THE WHARF

The man on the wharf, watching a man
shuck clams on the wharf, stands into

the wind as if he hung on a mooring.
Rolling drunk, his sea-legs are stable;

he watches the boats go out and come in.
He casts off himself when they sail;

when they harbor they harbor toward him.
Wherever they sail or haul herring,

the man on the wharf has already been.
His fogged eye telescopes ports,

and multiplies one clear woman.
Her breasts were islands to home on,

sea-marks off his home cove, until
last winter sank her. Skim-ice ate

at the wharf through March. Like cancer.
Or like a surgeon cutting through multiplication.

The man on the wharf cannot remember
which. Or why he stands into the wind,

watching a man shuck clams on the wharf,
watching as if his hand held the knife.

He watches himself watching, in mind
of his son who will not write him, cut

by the wind that quicks through his workshirt,
by sunlight glinting the waves like knives.

He pisses behind the boatshed, warm
where his body performs its remaining function;

then sucks at his pint of Jim Beam, relieved.
Rolled back into the wind again,

he watches the man shuck clams on the wharf.
He's almost calm, who swallows no answer,

but questions in bourbon this seeming harbor,
this harbor where he has always lived.

Distilled by an Indian sun, its hill-
sides bourbon, its trees thinned to rust,

it leaves him no choice of winters, no
skipper whose last command he might balk at,

now that the fishboats have cast him off.
They harbor downwind, rolling drunkenly

toward him.
                    The sea is all he can ask.

FIVE WAYS OF FACING THE ⌐

I. STEFANSSON ISLAND

Vilhjalmur Stefansson
(1879–1962)

Stefansson: a walrus of a man
whose walk is paced to sled dogs
on the offshore ice. Time drags
behind him now, but tundra sun
still lights the winter island
      of his mind.

Alaska blizzards drift his hair;
there is seal meat in him, the warmth
of blubber, a white bear's strength.
His eyelids tighten in the glare
of memory, the ranges of the Yukon
      map his skin.

As on the Beaufort Sea, where man
walks small across the frozen tides,
he in his glacial knowledge plods
to tame not barren lands to man,
but man to what is barren. Across
      the moving ice

he walked three months: Martin Point
to Norway Island, six hundred miles

by stars. Three men, six dogs, seals
to kill between the floes; and plant-
life on whatever shore, to prove
    how prayer may starve

a man where science can find food.
He is a hunter still, exiled
from the arctic night, yet reconciled
to shape a snowblind course. Outward
on mush ice he moves, with no fear
    of magnetic error.

No South can thaw this polar man.
But close to compass North, an island
maps his name: dovekies breed downwind
of his torn flag; the solstice sun
fires lichen into arctic bloom,
    beyond all word of him.

II. HOMAGE

Henry Moore
(1898–   )

As glaciers etched this island ledge
toward ebbing, the eye tracks its grain
to where granite slides into the sea.

As waves shallow and grind, figures
appear, released above the tideline.
They barely recline, often in family

groups, spaced by how winds find them.
The sun has gutted their loins; open
to every weather, they let cold fog

channel their hollows. Cast up
from generations of rock, they own
the residual life of bronze, stone, salt.

A man wades out to shape their name:
by how his gestures carve the wind,
they let the tide speak through their human

voids, awash in equal candor.
They understand. He understands.
And then, again, they go under.

III. A CHOICE OF HORIZONS

Andrew Wyeth
(1916–   )

A wind lifts hard
into the empty
room, a cold front
curtains the sun's
November ebb.

There's no down bed
to love on; a spit
of snow quilts into
the salt marshes,
crows narrow

the window and
widow the eye.
A fisherman's woman

hooks her body
uphill, angling

against the rip-
tide stubble; home
is a dressed-out buck
hung swinging behind
her woodshed wall.

A boy might saddle
his bicycle here,
and canter inland
along the flat
blacktop, as if

to outpump a sunk
dory, out-pedal
the wind, and shelter
behind some town
the man he must be.

But always over
the naked ridgepoles,
the salt-bleached shakes
and globed lightning rods,
the wind outlasts

his wind: he coasts
in mind of his dory,
a woman weathered
by storms, and the
sea, the sea, the sea.

IV. LIGHT

William Thon
(1906–   )

Thon sails light, self-taught
by the ache, dark, and wet of it;
he quarries how it cracks out

at sunset, cut like granite
lighted off islands: the weight,
the winter, the hurricane of it.

He waves it light as a fishnet
drying, the oil, its fishboat
roll, its fog and tidal set.

He harbors it at Port Clyde:
the cold seabird shape of it,
its neap, and quiet spring tide.

V. SEA-CHANGE

John Marin
(1870–1953)

Marin
saw how it feels:
the first raw shock
of Labrador current,
the surfacing gasp
at jut of rock,
bent sails, and wedged
trees. He wrote it:

Stonington, Small
Point, and Cape Split,
through a pane so
cracked by the lode-
star sun that he
swam back, blinded,
into himself to
sign the after-
image: initialed
mountains, ledged
towns (white as
Machias after
the hayrake rain),
sun-splintered
water and written
granite; dark light
unlike what you
ever saw until,
inland, your own
eyes close and, out
of that sea-change,
islands rise thick:
like the rip-tide
paint that, flooding,
tugs at your vitals,
and is more Maine
than Maine.

THE SEDGWICK BOULDER

It's elephant, big
as a fisherman's house,

its faces carved
with no mark of love,

but casually graved
by the hard patina

of weather. God
only knows what glacier

eased its grip
here; that history

of melting got dropped
when Sedgwick's Selectmen

rocked Town Meeting—
by having already

spent without Warrant
the price of an ill-

conceived road sign.
Maybe they'd still

be in office, repentant,
if fresh paint hadn't

set up to proclaim
that theirs, in its

alder clearing, was
only (forever)

*The Second Largest
Boulder in Maine.*

Maybe that's all
it is.   God

couldn't care less;
nor did those natives

who wouldn't vote.
The size of their rock

is no less or more
than the size of that shuttered

house by the shore
in which (without windows

or speech) the town's
new widows are locked

for a year and a moon.
Nobody needs

to bait traps to hear
what such women try

to ask about love;
the waves fish-in

on every old tide,
answering only

themselves. Even
kid-sisters new

to a Ford backseat
refuse to screw

in the clearing shadowed
by Sedgwick's great stone.

It feels like the anchor
cast, and then swallowed,

by all their sisters'
kid husbands when they,

come home from the sea,
gave lobstermen's thanks

to a lobsterman's God,
and then, rowing in

through the quick salt ice,
joked-home about bed

and love, to drown
in Sedgwick's one cove.

Maybe it was
for them that Sedgwick's

three Selectmen
were bent on raising

a sign that might mark
this speechless rock.

Whatever defense
they had, in fact,

for their spendthrift act,
the town never heard;

they went down at Town
Meeting the way

their sons sank: with-
out saying a word.

THE SHIP

Watches North of the tropics,
still dwarfed by the ocean that pocked
her iron plates, she's anchored herself

off Searsport; and swung on her hook
for a week's end, a salt-mile offshore.
Searsport's no liberty port;

it's barely a harbor: a wharf,
a tidal point of white houses,
thick with their cargo of snow.

Nobody local knows why
she's here, her fires apparently
banked, with only the rusted

top of her smokestack smudging
the frozen air. Talk says
that her crew's all sick, but men

on a catwalk bend to chip paint;
others stand watch on the wings
of her bridge in what, through binoc-

ulars, looks like health.
She's flown no quarantine flag;
no boat's put ashore for a doctor,

water, or food. Nobody's
even landed, in fact, to pay
some small respect to the Harbor-

master. Because of the rumor
of plague, he's ordered the fishboats
to stay in port. The windows

of every drowned grandfather's house
are busy with rumor's widows:
not so much watching the ship

herself as watching their husbands
congress the wharf. They all
agree, by her Plimsoll marks,

that she's slightly down by the bow,
perhaps because of the crates
on her foredeck. Still, she's shown

no sign of distress; although
her sheer is foreign, her lights
conform to International

Rules: the consensus is
that she isn't Russian. But no man
wakes in Searsport who doesn't

get up to look for her flag;
the women, had they a right word,
would pray some name on her transom.

If only she'd signal her business,
call *M'aidez!* or put in for help,
Searsport might ease its distress.

Searsport's sent more captains
to sea than any Maine port
in history; its children, even,

are baptized by disaster.
Yet even the town's most famous
son, a mutineer hung

in the crosstrees, could never
imagine an old tramp tired
of passage, who simply put in

in need of reflection at anchor.
Whatever port Searsport once was,
she found it no harbor-of-refuge;

after she'd lain here only
three days, and kept her own
silence from Friday through Sunday,

every white house and upright
church, self-exiled by anger,
prided itself with outrage.

Whatever her registry, tonnage,
or name, whatever it was
she came for, Searsport delivered

no goods to her hold and recovered
no profit from what she might light.
She stoked up her fires early

this morning, and weighed her great hook
before breakfast. Watching
her hull, and then her thin plume

of smoke, sink over the known
horizon, the town stood as close
to attention as Maine is ever,

with strangers, likely to get.
As long as men fish, her wake's
bound to roil the turned tide,

and churn the fogged bell
the fishboats bear on, sounding
their own thin horns to locate

each other. Until Searsport
melts, or the Bay freezes over,
the natives are liable to never

recover: denying this coast
as if it didn't exist,
the ship made raw her departure

around the Three Mile black buoy.
It's always been out there, seaward
of every quilt bed and the town's

five steeples: a secular bell
for the exiled ear to home on,
tended by gulls in its floating

cage, tolling both warning
and sea-room. Nobody paid it
much mind until this morning:

the ship, edging out, gave it
nine great blasts on her horn,
as if in familiar salute.

REFUSING THE SEA

I

As headlands weather a gale,
and barns sleep against weather,
the sea argues hemlock and rock.

Granite and dwarf-pine fend
against wind; the moon floods in
where the ebb tries to tack.

Tonight is nobody's harbor.
Make-and-break fishermen tide
themselves over: they lock

their nets on the groundswell bottom,
and plow offshore to ride
the night out. Their gunwales wash black

and roll clear: the helmsman's eye
is decked with moons. But everyman
fished in his forepeak hammock

sleeps like a gimbaled compass.
As herring survive who school
beyond coves and harbor wrack,

men slept hove-to over fifty
fathoms will, silvered by
fish-scales, net coming back.

II

The bellbuoy rang its tides
all night, banging its changes
against sleep's undertow.

At night in Maine, all night,
the wind climbs into the elms;
the stars revolve their slow

old pattern, turning the moon
to lure new schools of herring.
And we on Main Street, bloated

with heirloom rum, choke
on our fishbone nightmares: son
like father, we never boated

a fish, or gambled a widow
to cast for ourselves. We bank
in Boston, refusing the sea,

while men with Mediterranean
names gaff our daughters
to bed. Porpoises sport

the morning tide while we
tend shop on a chamber pot,
and settle our will in chancery.

VOYAGES

Butt-down on granite,
facing a weathered sea,
I breathe as slow as rock.

Harbor is one way to look;
but voyages wash my eye,
and old tides rock my butt.

Gulls root on the ledge,
taught by every wind
how spruces tug; snails

hug the tideline, hulls
on their own horizon: bound
as I am to the very edge.

REPORT FROM THE SCENE

*Severe local thunderstorms will
move into higher elevations late
this afternoon, and will reach
the coast by night.*

The harbor opens
and shuts in blue

electric flashes:
the dark is total,

the boats, white.
Quietly, under

the rivering thunder,
each in its turn

swings bow to the wind,
hung on a solo

mooring. The harbor
shutters and opens,

a camera remotely
focused on Jove's

apocalypse tricks.
Negatives of

ourselves, exposed
by each strike,

we feel for each other
with reflex love,

and almost see
what we look like.

SEAWEED

Ontogeny recapitulates phylogeny

Naked on island rock,
bodied with salt in the late
sun, we dry and look down:
golden wilds of seaweed
garden the dive we surfaced from.

Stripped to who we once were,
we submerged in the wash
of floodtide: man and bride,
we swam who we might become.
After the ebb taught us love

we climbed out of the sea;
but if there are seaweed gods
I think we are wed by them:
I feel salt still on your back,
your bones swim under me.

TENANTS' HARBOR

Listen, the tide has turned:
you can hear yesterday's left-
over swell, fooling around

against Condon's Rock. Who's
to care where the cold front went,
when it lifted a week of nimbus

clear of the Camden Hills?
Somebody's probably mapped
it, as part of a spiral,

current from Canso
to Gander; people are always
pulsing their plot of distance

from storms, from a weapons-system,
a star, or a war. Safe
from radar, we're eased home

by how the wind climbed out
of the cove, and leaned Orion
down to this summer's last night.

Tomorrow, counting our change
at a tollgate, we'll suck
on a hot inland orange

for lunch, gas up to anchor
ourselves to a map, and plot
the cost of a winter ashore.

Tonight we only chart
ourselves, in how through spruce
the thick stars constellate.

This side of Condon's Rock
we're tenant to two black ducks,
discussing themselves in the dark.

Who's to tell them the world
lies elsewhere? Not you,
nor I, who migrate. The world

is wherever we quiet to hear it.
Tides darken our listening;
comic as ducks, we share it.

OFFSHORE

The bay was anchor, sky,
and island: a land's end
sail, and the world tidal,
that day of blue and boat.

The island swam in the wind
all noon, a seal until
the sun furled down. Orion
loomed, that night, from unfathomed

tides; the flooding sky
was Baltic with thick stars.
On watch for whatever catch,
we coursed that open sea

as if by stars sailed off
the chart; we crewed with Arc-
turus, Vega, Polaris,
tacking into the dark.